I am a
RASTAFARIAN

I am a
RASTAFARIAN

Obadiah
meets
Petra Gaynor

Photography: Chris Fairclough

WATTS BOOKS
LONDON • NEW YORK • SYDNEY

Petra Gaynor is 8 years old. She and her family are Rastafarians. Her mother Sandra Gaynor is a member of the Ethiopian World Federation and dances in an African dance troupe. They live in Highgate, Birmingham, where Petra goes to school.

Contents

© 1984 Watts Books
Paperback edition 1993
This edition 1995

Watts Books
96 Leonard Street
London
EC2A 4RH

Franklin Watts Australia
14 Mars Road
Lane Cove
NSW 2066

ISBN 0 86313 260 X (hardback)
ISBN 0 7496 1408 0 (paperback)

The Publishers would like to
thank all the people shown
in this book.

Printed in Hong Kong

The Rastafarian belief

My family lives a way of life that has come to be called Rastafari.

Rastafari is a way of life, not a religion, which has many links with the Jewish and Christian faiths. It is named after Ras Tafari who became Emperor Haile Selassie I of Ethiopia in 1930. Rastafari, however, was begun in Jamaica in the 1920's but only got its name when Ras Tafari was proclaimed Emperor.

We worship Haile Selassie I as Jah Everliving. Jah is our name for God.

Rastafarians believe that Jah shows Himself in human form from time to time. It was prophesied in the 1920's that Jah would show himself as a Black King of Africa. He would help Black people to return home to Africa. Many had been removed by force from Africa during the course of the slave trade, which ended in the early nineteenth century. Emperor Haile Selassie I was seen as this King. Rastafarians are guided by the culture and traditions of Ethiopia.

HAILE SELASSIE I
Emperor of Ethiopia

Going to a Meeting

We are members of the Ethiopian World Federation. When we go to the weekly Meeting we are met by the Sergeant-at-Arms.

The Sergeant-at-Arms makes sure that all adults sign the security book. Before entering the room all the male members must remove their hats. The Ethiopian World Federation was established in 1937 by Emperor Haile Selassie I. The weekly Meeting is both a spiritual and business occasion. It covers all aspects of day to day life.

We do not have a church or building of our own, so we go to a local community hall. The Chaplain leads the service.

The Chaplain is elected for one year and has special duties such as visiting the sick. He opens each meeting with the Ethiopian National Anthem and then leads the congregation in song, prayer and music. The spiritual part of the Meeting lasts for about twenty minutes.

The Business Meeting

After the hymns and prayers there is a Business Meeting. The Elders make sure that we are all being looked after.

The main purpose of the weekly Business Meeting is to plan everyday duties and special events. There are several committees covering such topics as education and money. Representatives come and report to the membership on their work. The Chaplain reports also to the Sick Committee. They also make plans for festivals and celebrations.

The Meetings are lively as there is always plenty to talk about. The Chairperson keeps order.

A wide range of activities are planned at the Meetings. These include cultural evenings with speakers, dance and drama events. They also plan the Bible Study classes and activities during the children's holiday time. These Meetings always end with prayers and drumming.

The history of Rastafari

Marcus Garvey is our Prophet. He foretold that a King would be crowned in Africa who would save and redeem Black people.

Marcus Garvey was born in Jamaica in 1887. He believed that Black people were still suffering from the effects of slavery. Emperor Haile Selassie I was later seen as the King prophesied by Marcus Garvey. Marcus Garvey organized thousands of Black people in Jamaica and America by encouraging unity and pride in their African heritage.

St. George Cathedral, Addis Ababa where H.I.M. was crowned

I like to hear the story which tells how Haile Selassie I is descended from King Solomon of Israel.

Solomon, Son of David, became known for the wisdom with which he ruled his country. Makeda, Queen of Sheba, journeyed from Ethiopia to meet Solomon. They had a son called Menelik. Haile Selassie I is 225th in the line of Solomon. When he became Emperor, he was given the title "King of Kings, Elect of God, Conquering Lion of the tribe of Judah."

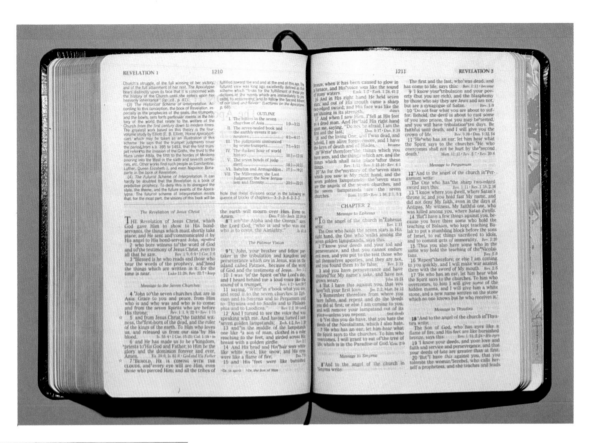

The Holy Book and symbols

I know many Bible stories, especially from the Old Testament.

Rastafarians study the Bible. Christianity became the official religion of Ethiopia in 330 A.D. They pay particular attention to the teaching of the Old Testament. They study all 87 books including the Apochrypha and the Book of Enoch. The Authorized Version used by many Christian Churches has 66 books.

We hold our hands in a special way when we pray. We must not cut our hair.

The shape of the hands when praying is a symbol for both peace and war. It represents a heart and a spear. In the Bible God told the Nazarites, a group of ancient Israelites, to keep their hair natural and un-cut. Rastafarians keep this covenant or agreement with Jah. It is a symbol of physical and moral strength. Their distinctive braids are called dreadlocks. Crosses are seen as symbols of the burden of life.

The history of Petra's family

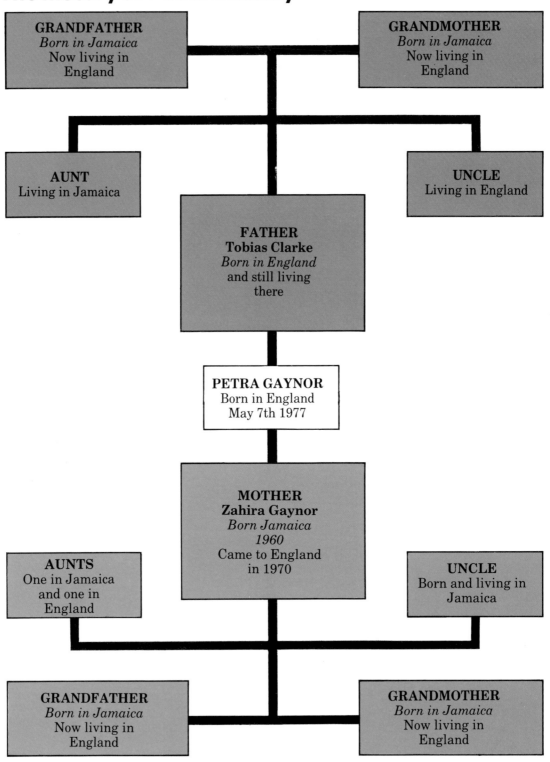

GRANDFATHER
Born in Jamaica
Now living in
England

GRANDMOTHER
Born in Jamaica
Now living in
England

AUNT
Living in Jamaica

UNCLE
Living in England

FATHER
Tobias Clarke
Born in England
and still living
there

PETRA GAYNOR
Born in England
May 7th 1977

MOTHER
Zahira Gaynor
Born Jamaica
1960
Came to England
in 1970

AUNTS
One in Jamaica
and one in
England

UNCLE
Born and living in
Jamaica

GRANDFATHER
Born in Jamaica
Now living in
England

GRANDMOTHER
Born in Jamaica
Now living in
England

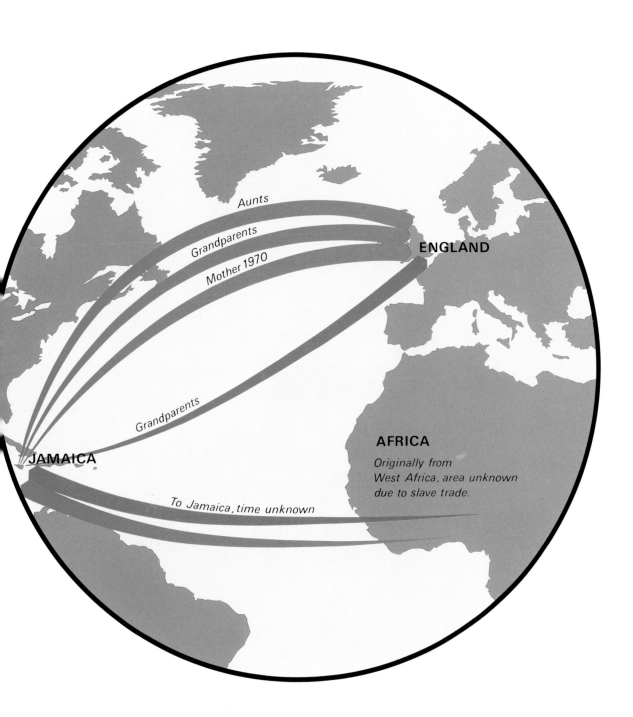

What Rastafarians wear

I always wear something to cover my head. When I wear the Ethiopian style scarf my mother wraps it round for me.

Rastafarians usually keep their heads covered. Females must cover their heads during a Meeting, particularly when the congregation is praying. Knitted hats called tams are popular with males and females. Their design often includes the yellow, red, green and black of the Ethiopian flag.

 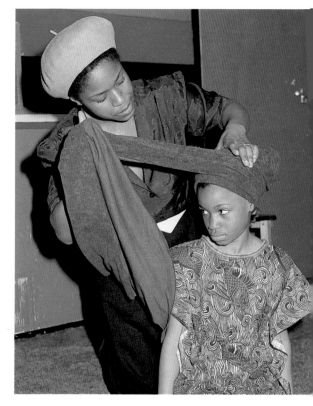

My mother has made me some clothes using traditional African prints. Traditional Ethiopian clothes are sometimes worn on Holy Days.

Rastafarians do not usually place much importance on clothes. Simple styles are most liked. There is, however, much interest in African dress and sometimes these clothes are worn for special occasions such as festivals. In Ethiopia white is worn on Holy Days, though this is not done so much in the West.

Eating the Rastafarian way

My family is vegetarian. When we go shopping my mother checks the packets to make sure no animal fats are in the food.

Most Rastafarians are vegetarians though some will eat fish. The most orthodox eat no eggs or dairy foods. Rastafarians, like other Afro-Caribbean people, eat a mixture of Caribbean and other foods. There are grocery shops and markets in large cities, where Caribbean fruits and vegetables can always be bought.

At school I am not the only vegetarian. Some of my friends do not eat meat either.

Rastafarians have needed to find out about different foods and are interested in nutrition and a healthy diet. They believe that this is an important part of a natural and healthy lifestyle. Specialist health food shops provide many essential groceries. Pork and unscaled fish are never eaten. These rules are found in the Old Testament.

Rastafarian music

I enjoy listening to the music played at the weekly meeting and on special occasions. Drummers make their own drums using metal bars and goatskin.

Drumming is an important part of the African heritage of Rastafarians. The drummers accompany hymns and songs as well as dances. In Africa the drums are made from tree trunks. In the Caribbean a different way was found using old barrels from cargo ships.

There is a big and small drum which I have seen played. They make different sounds. When we are at home we sometimes listen to reggae music.

There are three main drums. These are the bass, fundie and repeater. When Rastafarians come together to drum and chant it is called Nyahbinghi. Reggae music is built on the same foundation as Nyahbinghi. Through reggae Rastafarians sing about their beliefs and the social conditions they live in.

Festivals

I go to all the main festivals with my family. I like watching the dancers.

On Holy Days, cultural festivals are arranged by the community. Rastafarians are interested in the traditions and culture of all African countries. There are many dance troupes in England now and they perform all over Great Britain. At other times, visiting Elders give lectures or films may be shown.

There are many things to see at the festivals such as posters and paintings. My mother always buys me something to take home.

The Ethiopian New Year, Haile Selassie's Birthday and Coronation are the main celebrations held. Many also like to celebrate Marcus Garvey's birthday. These are all occasions when the family will take part. The children can often join in dancing with the adults. There are also drama sessions for children. There are often art exhibitions and vegetarian food is available.

Arts and Crafts

In our house we have many things made by Rastafarians.

Arts and crafts are an important activity. Products are usually made from natural materials. Badges and bowls are made from coconut shell and plaques from wood. There are many beautiful Rastafarian paintings. Dreadlocks, slavery, Haile Selassie I and Marcus Garvey are popular subjects. The red, green, yellow and black of the Ethiopian flag are often included in paintings.

Amharic is the language of Ethiopia. I go to a special class to learn how to write it.

Amharic is the most commonly used language in Ethiopia today. Until Haile Selassie I became ruler, the most important written language was called Ge'ez. This was used in all official documents and books. It was not easily understood by ordinary people. Amharic is now the official language of Ethiopia although Ge'ez is still used by the Ethiopian orthodox Christian Church.

Amharic Script

ጥ ቁር
(Tikur)
BLACK

መጽሐፍ ቅዱስ
(Mets-Haf Kioous)
HOLY BIBLE

ሻ ይ
(Shayi)
TEA

The Rastafarian Year

The Ethiopian calendar is used by Rastafarians. This has 13 months in a year and begins on September 11th. The last month of the year has only six days. Each year is named after one of the apostles— Matthew, Mark, Luke and John.

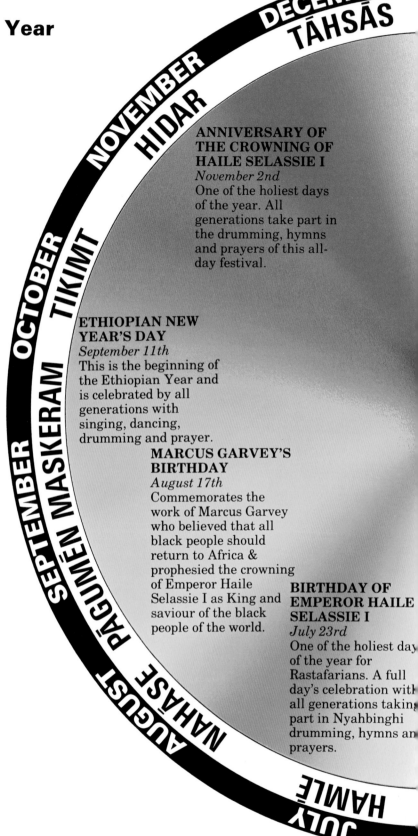

ANNIVERSARY OF THE CROWNING OF HAILE SELASSIE I
November 2nd
One of the holiest days of the year. All generations take part in the drumming, hymns and prayers of this all-day festival.

ETHIOPIAN NEW YEAR'S DAY
September 11th
This is the beginning of the Ethiopian Year and is celebrated by all generations with singing, dancing, drumming and prayer.

MARCUS GARVEY'S BIRTHDAY
August 17th
Commemorates the work of Marcus Garvey who believed that all black people should return to Africa & prophesied the crowning of Emperor Haile Selassie I as King and saviour of the black people of the world.

BIRTHDAY OF EMPEROR HAILE SELASSIE I
July 23rd
One of the holiest day of the year for Rastafarians. A full day's celebration with all generations taking part in Nyahbinghi drumming, hymns and prayers.

DECEMBER TĀHSĀS
NOVEMBER HIDAR
OCTOBER TIKIMT
SEPTEMBER MASKERAM
PĀGUMĒN
AUGUST NĀHASĒ
JULY HAMLĒ

JANUARY
TIR

FEBRUARY
YAKĀTIT

MARCH
MAGGABIT

APRIL
MIYĀZYĀ

MAY
GINBOT

JUNE
SANÉ

ETHIOPIAN CHRISTMAS
January 7th
Although this is not a celebration of Jesus' birthday, it is an acknowledgement of his life and works.

ETHIOPIAN CONSTITUTION DAY
July 16th
Commemorates the granting of Ethiopia's first Constitution in 1931 by His Imperial Majesty Haile Selassie I.

29

Facts and Figures

Rastafari people can be found in many countries of the world. These include Jamaica and most other Caribbean Islands, England, U.S.A., Canada, Europe, South America, Australia and many African Countries.

The Rastafari movement first started in Jamaica in the early 1920's. Marcus Garvey had prophesied the crowning of a Black King and had formed the United Negro Improvement Association. Many people began to look to Africa. Among them were Leonard Howell, J.N Hibbert and Archibald Dunkley, who were the first to preach of the divinity of Ras Tafari.

Haile Selassie I was born on July 23, 1892 and crowned Emperor on Nov 2, 1930 in Addis Ababa, capital city of Ethiopia. He was 225th in line from King Solomon, the son of David of Israel. This dynasty was established in Ethiopia by Menelik I, son of Solomon and Queen Makeda of Sheba.

The lion is the imperial symbol of Ethiopia. It was used on many things such as banknotes, during the reign of Haile Selassie I. To Rastafarians the lion symbolizes strength and power.

The Ethiopian World Federation Inc. was founded in New York, U.S.A. by Dr Malaku E. Bayen, by order of his Imperial Majesty Haile Selassie I of Ethiopia on August 25, 1937. It was formed to help support Ethiopia after it had been invaded by Italy.

Orthodox Nyahbinghi Rastafarians believe in:
– One true God, Haile Selassie I of Ethiopia.
– The return to their true home in Africa, after being freed from the evils of the Western World, more often called Babylon.
– The destruction of Oppression.

Rastafarians have developed their own word system which is used in everyday speech. The letter 'I' is used to show the oneness with Jah. It replaces the beginning of many words to give better expression. Some common words are:
Irits – spirits
Ily – holy
Iscience – conscience
Iower – power
Ital – vital (food)

Glossary

Amharic The Ethiopian national language.

Bass One of the Nyahbinghi drums. It represents the sound of thunder.

Chairperson The person elected to keep order at a Meeting.

Chaplain One who looks after the spiritual needs of the members.

Dreadlocks The uncombed and matted braids of Rastafarians.

Elder A person of high standing or old age in Rastafarian society.

Fundie Nyahbinghi drum representing the sound of an earthquake.

Ge'ez An ancient language of Ethiopia still used by scholars.

Haile Selassie I Emperor of Ethiopia. Worshipped as Jah Everliving. His name means Power of the Trinity.

Ital a natural vegetarian way of living and eating.

Marcus Garvey A prophet who foretold the coming of a Black King. Leader of the Universal Negro Improvement Association.

Meeting A gathering of brothers and sisters in drumming and song.

Nazarites Ancient Israelites who made an agreement with God not to cut their hair.

Nyahbinghi An order, believed to have been founded by Haile Selassie I, which is pledged to end oppression in any society – Black or White. It is symbolized in Rastafari by drumming and chanting.

Ras Tafari The title of Haile Selassie I before he became Emperor. "Ras" means prince or head and "Tafari" means creator.

Reggae Musical form which began in Jamaica. Through it Rastafarians sing about the oppression of Black people.

Repeater Drum of the Nyahbinghi. It represents the sound of lightning.

Vegetarian A person who eats no animal flesh.

Vegan A vegetarian who eats no dairy products or eggs and who will not wear any articles of clothing made from animal products.

Index